T0068174

CLOSER TO GOD

Basics Like ABC'S

DEBORAH BOHLMAN DECKER

WESTBOW
PRESS®
A DIVISION OF THOMAS NELSON
& ZONDERVAN

WestBow Press books may be ordered through
booksellers or by contacting:

WestBow Press
A Division of Thomas Nelson & Zondervan
1663 Liberty Drive
Bloomington, IN 47403
www.westbowpress.com
844-714-3454

Scripture taken from the King James Version of the Bible.

ISBN: 978-1-6642-5881-5 (sc)
ISBN: 978-1-6642-5883-9 (hc)
ISBN: 978-1-6642-5882-2 (e)

Library of Congress Control Number: 2022903385

Print information available on the last page.

WestBow Press rev. date: 3/28/2022

Dedicated to my grandchildren: Ben Brown and Evangeline Brown. To my children: Matt Decker, Paul Decker, and Theresa Brown.

Special thanks to Alma Lomax, Tracy Bohlman, and Linda Gale.

Alma helped me type my first draft and encouraged me. She has been a true blessing in my life since we taught kindergarten along with Sabrina, Gloria,and Ann Marie.

Tracy is my cousin who keeps in touch everyday with encouraging words and inspirations.

Linda is a friend from way back to when we were 12. We have helped one another through the years and we have grown in God's grace and wisdom.

INTRODUCTION

You can add your own words that help you see God's characteristics and add Bible verses to relate.

I hope this helps with your daily walk with God.

If we want to spend eternity with God, we need to know something about Him.

I do not claim this to be a best or only way to get closer to God, but it has helped me and I hope it helps you too.

You can use the blank pages for photos or small memory items that remind you of God's love and blessings.

A

GOD IS ALMIGHTY

God is the creator and sustainer with Angel Armies, God knows all and has power over all.

As His child, I can trust God to help me through my day!
What a sense of peace and a reason to feel strong enough to handle whatever comes one day at a time. God does not want us to worry, but have faith in Him.

Revelation 1:8. I am the Alpha and Omega the beginning and ending, saith the Lord which is and was and is to come the Almighty.

Your notes

B

GOD BLESSES US

God has blessed us with a beautiful world with flowers, trees, birds, and amazing critters.

God has blessed us with oceans, rivers, lakes, and streams, and with mountains, forests and meadows.

God blesses us with family, friends, and a church home.

God blesses us with our health, our home and our finances.

As a child of God, I need to be a good steward and use wisely His blessings. When we think of God's blessings we can grow in an attitude of gratitude.

Proverbs 10:22.

Job 37:14. Consider the wondrous works of God.

Your notes

_____

_____

_____

_____

_____

_____

_____

_____

_____

_____

_____

_____

_____

_____

C

GOD CARES FOR ME

God is not distant. He is aware of our needs. God wants us to be in a caring relationship with Him, a daily walk and following His commandments. So, whatever our concerns, we can ask and receive those things that fit His will. God cares when we need courage, strength, and wisdom.

As a child of God, I need to care for others, I need to leave my concerns with the Lord. Everyday we can thank God for opportunities to say and do things that show caring.

Colossians 3:17.

I Peters 5:7. Casting all your cares upon Him, for He cares for you.

Hebrews 13:5b

Your notes

D

GOD DEFENDS AND DELIVERS

God keeps us from some problems, but those problems that come in our life; God is with us and helping to defend us.

As a child of God, I can always praise Him for His support. I might not know the issues God has prevented from happening, but I can take comfort in His watching over me. I can be confident that God will see me through all life's struggles as I trust Him.

Isaiah 41:10. Fear not; for I am with you, be not dismayed, for I am your God: I will strengthen you, I will help you, yes I will uphold you with the right hand of my righteousness.

Psalms 32:7

Your notes

E

GOD IS ETERNAL

God is forever and we cannot understand all.

We know our life here is short compared to eternity.

As a child of God, I must do all I can to encourage others and bring God's love to others. Time is to be used wisely and obeying God and following His will not my own selfish ways.

Revelation 1:8. I am the Alpha and the Omega.

Hebrews 13:8.

Your notes

_____

_____

_____

_____

_____

_____

_____

_____

_____

_____

_____

_____

_____

_____

F

GOD IS FAITH AND FORGIVENESS

God is faithful and He wants us to be faithful to Him,

God has made a way for our sins to be forgiven through Jesus who died for our sins—the perfect Lamb sacrifice.

As a child of God, I must seek to be faithful to God daily and ask for my forgiveness and for me to forgive others.
We need to accept God's plan for forgiveness through faith in Jesus, so we can be close to God.

I Corinthians 2:5

I John 5:4. For what is born of God overcomes the world; and this is the victory that overcomes the world, even our faith.
Ephesians 4:32. Be kind to one another, tenderhearted, forgiving one another, even as God for Christ's sake has forgiven you.

Your notes

_____

_____

_____

_____

_____

_____

_____

_____

_____

_____

_____

_____

_____

_____

_____

G

GOD IS GRACE AND GLORY

God is worthy of all glory and He gives us grace.

As a child of God, I want my words and actions to reflect God's grace and give God the glory He so deserves.

Psalms 19:14

II Corinthians. 12:9, 10. My grace is sufficient for you. When I am weak; then I am strong.

Your notes

_____

_____

_____

_____

_____

_____

_____

_____

_____

_____

_____

_____

_____

_____

GOD IS HOLY AND OUR HOPE

God is Holy and His ways are beyond our understanding.

As a child of God, when life does not make sense; we have hope that our Holy God sees the whole picture. He will help us through all situations.. We do not need to know why but we know the who gives us hope in all our circumstances.

Psalms 145:17. The Lord is righteous in all His ways, and Holy in all his works.

Isaiah 55:8.

Revelation4:8

Your notes

_____

_____

_____

_____

_____

_____

_____

_____

_____

_____

_____

_____

_____

_____

I

GOD IS INFINITE

God can hear all the prayers and see all of His children at all times.

As a child of God, I can pray anywhere and anytime and know God is listening and seeing my needs. We can find faith, hope, love, peace, and joy, when we pray.

I John 3:22.

I John 5:14. This is the confidence that we have in Him, that if we ask anything according to His will, He hears us.

Your notes

_____

_____

_____

_____

_____

_____

_____

_____

_____

_____

_____

_____

_____

_____

J

GOD IS A JUST JUDGE

God has expectations for His children and when we fall short of what we know we should have done or should not have done; God wants us to ask forgiveness and help. We can be seen as pure in heart when we come before His judgement day. We will be all that we could be for Him.

As a child of God, I ask for forgiveness and the strength to listen and follow the Holy Spirit, God's helper within.

Psalms 26:1. Judge me oh Lord for I have walked in my integrity. I have trusted the Lord so I should not slide.

Your notes

_____

_____

_____

_____

_____

_____

_____

_____

_____

_____

_____

_____

_____

_____

K

GOD HAS A KINGDOM

God's Kingdom is where we want to live forever. We want to encourage one another to live this life as in His kingdom.

As a child of God, I need to make each day count to encourage others to seek God and His Kingdom.

Hebrews 12:28. Wherefore we receive the kingdom which can not be moved. Let us have grace whereby we may serve God acceptably with reverence and Godly fear.

Your notes

_____

_____

_____

_____

_____

_____

_____

_____

_____

_____

_____

_____

_____

_____

L

GOD IS LOVE

God is love and He listens. We know God loves us because He tells us. He helps us. He spends time with us. He blesses us.

As a child of God, I need to live lovingly and be a listener.

Timothy 1:7. For God has not given us the spirit of fear, but of power and of love and a sound mind.

Daniel 9:17.

Hebrews10:24

I John 5:14.

Your notes

_____

_____

_____

_____

_____

_____

_____

_____

_____

_____

_____

_____

_____

M

GOD IS MERCIFUL, A MIRACLE WORKER AND A MIGHTY GOD

God's mercy reaches us through miracles sometimes.

As a child of God, I can attempt things that seem like more than I can do.

Deuteronomy 10:17. The Lord your God is God of Gods, and Lord of Lords, a great God; mighty and awe-inspiring.

Psalms 37
Jerimiah 33:11

GOD IS MERCIFUL, A MIRACLE WORKER AND A MIGHTY GOD

Your notes

N

GOD IS NON PARTISAN

God does not respect you for the money you have, the education you have, or the groups that you are in, and certainly not by the color of your skin. God respects a heart that seeks a daily walk with Him and a desire to serve Him.

As a child of God, I should not judge others, and I should respect a Godly character (as shown by the fruits of the spirit-love, joy, peace, patience, gentleness, goodness, faith, meekness, and self control.)

Romans 10:12. There is no difference between the Jew and the Greek; for the same Lord overall is rich unto all that call upon Him.

Your notes

_____

_____

_____

_____

_____

_____

_____

_____

_____

_____

_____

_____

_____

_____

O

GOD WANT US TO OBEY

God has commandments and He wants us to willingly obey.

As a child of God, I want to be obedient and I can ask for help, when it is difficult.

Colossians 3:17. Whatever you do in word or deed, do all in the name of Jesus giving thanks to God, the Father by Him.

Colossians 3:23. 8

Your notes

_____

_____

_____

_____

_____

_____

_____

_____

_____

_____

_____

_____

_____

_____

P

GOD IS PEACE

God can fill our soul with His peace—if we do not fill our spirit with worry.

As a child of God, I can find peace each day with God.

Philippians 4:6-7. Be anxious for nothing, but in everything by prayer and supplication with thanksgiving let your requests be made known to God, And the peace of God which passes all understanding shall keep your hearts and mind through Christ Jesus,

Note: Please know that some anxiety or depression needs professional help and let prayer direct you to find the best help.

Your notes

Q

GOD LIKES QUIET

God like a good parent does not like to shout at us but speaks to us in a quiet voice.

As a child of God, I need to make time for quiet.

I Thessalonians 4:11. Study to be quiet, Work with your own hands as we commanded you. That you may walk honestly to them that are without and you may lack nothing.

Your notes

R

GOD IS RIGHTEOUS AND HE GIVES US REST TO RESTORE US.

God makes us humble. We respect His greatness. God gives time to rest and be restored. God is righteous.

As a child of God, I need to rest in God and let Him restore my brokenness.

Psalms 21:3. He restores my soul. He leads me in the path of righteousness for His namesake.

Your notes

_____

_____

_____

_____

_____

_____

_____

_____

_____

_____

_____

_____

_____

S

GOD SENT JESUS FOR SALVATION, THE HOLY SPIRIT FOR SPIRITUAL GROWTH, AND HE SENDS OPPORTUNITIES TO SERVE.

God is a sender of what we need: Salvation, the Helper, and chances to serve.

As a child of God, I need to accept salvation, live in God's will, with the helper and serve God as I can.

John 3:16. For God so loved the world, that He gave His only begotten son, that whosoever believes in Him should not perish, but have everlasting life.

John 14:16. I will pray to the Father and He will give you another comforter that He may abide with you forever.

Galatians 6:9.

Your notes

T

GOD IS TRUTH

God is truth. We can trust Him. God's truth has perfect timing and when we are tested; we know God will give us a testimony.

As a child of God, I trust God's truth, I know His timing is perfect. He helps me through all tasks.

Psalms 25:5. Lead me in thy truths and teach me for thou art the God of my salvation: on you do I wait all the day.

Your notes

U

GOD IS UNSTOPPABLE AND UNCHANGING

God has some purposed plans that will not change or will be stopped. God does not change but His nature to listen to intercessory prayer can change events.

As a child of God, my love of God needs to be unmovable.

I Corinthians 15:58. Be steadfast, unmovable, always abounding in the work of the Lord, you know your labor is not in vain.

Hebrews 1:12b.

Your notes

_____

_____

_____

_____

_____

_____

_____

_____

_____

_____

_____

_____

_____

_____

V

GOD HAS A VISION FOR US.

God is the vine and I am the branch. God has a plan for each life—we may choose to go our own way, but like a good father God welcomes us back to Him as we repent. God is the vine and I am the branch getting my life needs from Him.

As a child of God, I need to read the Bible and pray and let the Holy Spirit guide me to God's will and not my will.

Romans 8:28. 31. All things work together for good to them that love God. If God is for us, who can be against us.

John 15:5. I am the true vine and you are the branches. He that abides in me and I in him, but the same bring forth much fruit, for without me you can do nothing.

Your notes

W

GOD IS ALL WISDOM, WORTHY OF OUR WORSHIP

God provides wisdom—our church should shine a light on His word and give us a way to serve. God deals with us as individuals, but He wants us to worship and serve Him through his church—together we can do more.

As a child of God, I ask daily for wisdom to make daily decisions. I pray I can worship daily.

1 Corinthians 1:24.

Psalms 95:6.

Proverbs 2:60. For the Lord gives wisdom out of His mouth comes knowledge and understanding.

Your notes

_____

_____

_____

_____

_____

_____

_____

_____

_____

_____

_____

_____

_____

_____

X

GOD LIKE AN X-RAY KNOWS OUR HEALTH.

God is aware of our body the temple of His Holy Spirit.

As a child of God, I take care of my body and do those things that are pleasing to God.

1 Corinthians 6:19. Your body is the temple of the Holy Spirit which is in you.

Your notes

_____

_____

_____

_____

_____

_____

_____

_____

_____

_____

_____

_____

_____

_____

_____

Y

GOD HAS PROMISES FOR YOU

God knows us and our needs and makes promises for you and yours.

As a child of God, I need to remember His promises and listen to His warnings. God promises His presence, His provision for us, His plans for us and His peace with Him.

Hebrews 13:5b.

Philippians 4:19.

Proverbs3:5-6. Trust in the Lord with all your heart and lean not into your own understanding. In all your ways acknowledge Him and He will direct your path.

Your notes

Z

GOD IS ZEAL, ENTHUSIASM AND JOY

God has zeal and enthusiasm and joy for all that love Him.

As a child of God, I should radiate his joy!

Romans 10:20. I bear records that they have the zeal of God.

Your notes

_____

_____

_____

_____

_____

_____

_____

_____

_____

_____

_____

_____

_____

_____

ABOUT THE AUTHOR

I am Deborah Bohlman Decker a mother of 3 and Nana to 2 children. I am not a professional writer, but a person who wants to leave a legacy of faith to my family.

I started my ABC's of God's attributes as a way to fall asleep. This still works as,thinking about God, helps me get comfortable and sleep comes naturally.

I eventually wrote my ABC's down. I use these in my daily devotional time. Most days I go through all the letters but sometimes I focus on a letter that fits my thoughts or needs

I am thankful for all those who have helped me grow spiritually throughout my life. As a child I looked up to my brother Gene and since he went to church, I wanted to go too. While sitting on a pew at a young age-maybe 10, I felt God calling me to work with children. At an earlier age maybe 4,

I would sit under the eaves where I could hear the rain and fold papers to make a book-scribbles to everyone but me. I became a teacher and I did a lot of volunteer work, but only now in my seventies am I attempting my early interest in writing.

God helped me through out my life. I was dedicated as a baby, and was sprinkled baptized at my church near my home. Eventually I taught Sunday School and created a program for mixed ages. When I moved to Georgia with my husband Phil I got baptized by dunking in a baptismal and I truly dedicated my life to Jesus.

Before I was married and moved to Georgia I went to college- Westfield State and graduated with a teaching degree. I was not able to get a teaching position- I wanted to question God, but I kept trusting. I took a job at a nursing home. Before I moved to Georgia my dad got sick and because of my nursing home work- I could handle the problems and his death. When we moved I had no problem getting a teaching position. God had a plan and perfect timing.